Coping with Life

Finding Joy in Dealing with Troubles

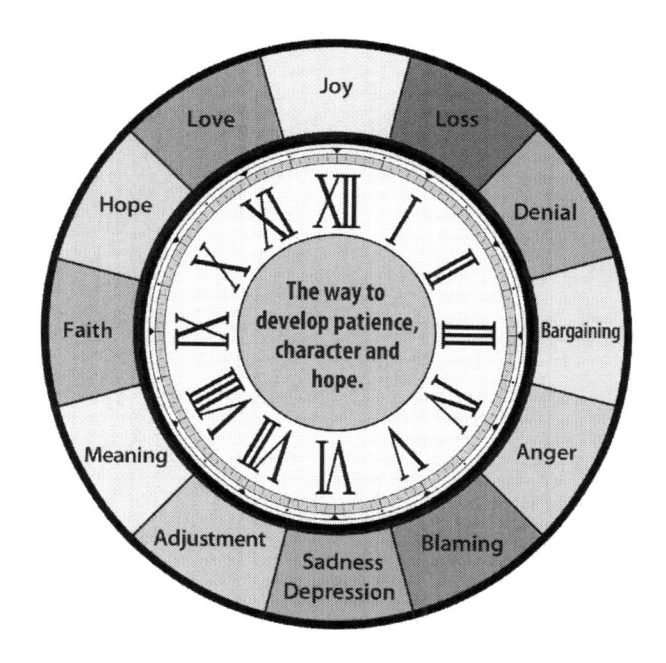

Harold Vann, MD
Author

Published by Harold Vann Books
February 2014

Printed by CreateSpace

Welcome to the challenge of being joyful when you meet various troubles in life since that is the way you will develop patience, character and hope.

Copyright Information

Copyright © 2014 by Harold F Vann of text and graphics. Presented by Amazon.com in digital format and in paperback. Developed using CreateSpace. All rights reserved, you have permission to quote paragraphs from this work providing you cite the source and the availability of copies on Amazon.com.

Scripture quotations designated ASV are taken from American Standard Version which is now in Public Domain. There are 16 verses quoted from ASV.

Scripture quotations taken from the 21st Century King James Version®, copyright © 1994 are designated by KJ21. Used by permission of Deuel Enterprises, Inc., Gary, SD 57237. All rights reserved. There are 12 verses quoted from KJ21.

Scripture quotations marked NIV are taken from THE HOLY BIBLE, NEW INTERNATIONAL VERSION®, NIV® COPYRIGHT ® 1973, 1978, 1984, 2011 by Biblica, Inc. ® Used by permission. All rights reserved worldwide. There are 30 verses quoted from NIV.

Scripture quotations marked NLT are taken from the Holy Bible, New Living Translation, copyright © 1996, 2004, 2007 by Tyndale House Foundation. Used by permission of Tyndale House Publishers, Inc., Carol Stream, Illinois 60188. All rights reserved. There are 46 verses quoted from NLT.

Scripture quotations marked MSG were taken from The Message, Copyright © 1993, 1994, 1995, 1996 2000, 2001, 2002. Used by permission of NavPress Publishing Group.
There are 13 verses quoted from MSG.

ISBN-13: 978-1495455216
ISBN-10: 149545521

Contents

		Page
Copyright Information		2
Author's Page		4
Introduction		5
Chapter		
I	Losses	10
	Physical, mental and spiritual losses will be a significant part of your life.	
II	Denial	13
	Denial is the first and may be the most frequently used mechanism in coping.	
III	Bargaining	15
	Be dependable in keeping your part of the bargain.	
IV	Anger	18
	Be angry and sin not.	
V	Blaming	22
	If you say you are perfect, watch out!	
VI	Sadness/Depression	24
	Bad things happen to good people.	
VII	Adjusting	28
	Be thankful, the Lord is near.	
VIII	Meaning	31
	What is God's purpose for you?	
IX	Faith	40
	Believe and not doubt, God is.	
X	Hope	44
	What do you hope for?	
XI	Love	47
	Love is the greatest spiritual gift.	
XII	Joy	51
	It is wonderful for us to be here.	
Acknowledgements		54
Coping Clock graphic for external use		57

Author's Page

This book is the result of my visiting men in jail who needed rehabilitation. As I helped them learn to find joy in spite of their troubles I developed this approach based on scriptures. After proving it I decided to share it with all who will use it.

I am a retired physician but am no longer licensed to practice medicine. I am not recommending any medical procedures, drugs or remedies but am sharing my experiences.

As I finished the draft, I thought of a number of things that I think could be helpful. So, perhaps I will do a second edition. You are welcome to email me with your suggestions at a specifically designated email address: copingmitlife@aol.com
If several of you contact me I will develop a blog on which to share experiences.

From time to time I will post comments concerning this book on my web page: www.copingwithlife.com

Harold Vann, MD

Introduction

Fellow sufferers, we are challenged to be extremely joyful when we have troubles of any kind. How can we be joyful when we face temptations, trials, tests, challenges, troubles or tribulations? James challenges us,

> "Dear brothers and sisters, when troubles come your way, consider it an opportunity for great joy. For you know that when your faith is tested, your endurance has a chance to grow. So let it grow, for when your endurance is fully developed, you will be perfect and complete, needing nothing" James 1:2-4, New Living Translation (NLT).

Then I read that Paul advised the same in Romans 5. Paul wrote,

> "Therefore, since we have been made right in God's sight by faith, we have peace with God because of what Jesus Christ our Lord has done for us. Because of our faith, Christ has brought us into this place of undeserved privilege where we now stand, and we confidently and joyfully look forward to sharing God's glory. We can rejoice, too, when we run into problems and trials, for we know that they help us develop endurance. And endurance develops strength of character, and character strengthens our confident hope of salvation. And this hope will not lead to disappointment. For we know how dearly God loves us, because he has given us the Holy Spirit to fill our hearts with his love" Romans 5:1-5 NLT.

I began to study both of these scriptures and came to the conclusion that if James and Paul were inspired to recommend we find joy in troubles I should pay attention. Soon I remembered how physical exercise with the resultant muscle soreness is required to perfect our muscle strength. This concept of "no pain, no gain" made sense.

It makes sense, but can I really feel joyful when the dermatologist tells my wife she needs an extensive operation to be sure her skin cancer is completely removed? We can be joyful even as we suffer once we realize this is the way we develop patience, character and hope. That is our great challenge, to do the hard suffering when necessary.

You may think "why welcome trouble?" The fact is that we will not need to look for trouble. It will come. Our challenge is to deal with trouble in the best way we can.

At this point I suggest that you keep your favorite Bible translation open as we refer to the scriptures.

We can use the clock to help us remember the stages in this process. If we imagine loss placed at one o'clock, denial at 2, bargaining at 3, anger at 4, blaming at 5, sadness at 6, adjustment at 7, meaning at 8, faith at 9, hope at 10, love at 11 and joy at 12 o'clock, we have an excellent mnemonic for these God-given mental and spiritual mechanisms of dealing with losses.

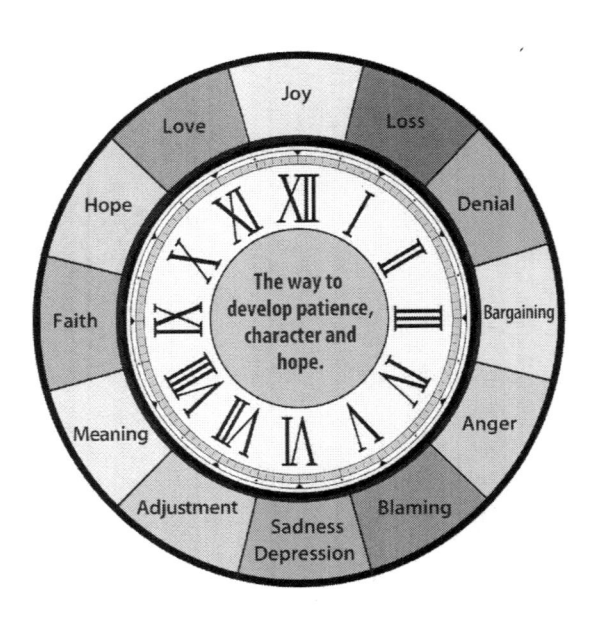

As you look at the specific stages you will discover many scriptures which apply. In Genesis Chapter 3 Adam & Eve practiced denial and blaming. In Genesis 18 Abraham bargained with God over the destruction of Sodom and Gomorrah. In Mark 3 Jesus expressed anger in the temple. The story of Job covers sadness extremely well. Philippians 4 deals with finding meaning in life. James 1 deals with adjusting to losses. Hebrews 11 is the basic text on faith. Hope is dealt with in Romans 8. The most valuable of the spiritual gifts is well described in I Corinthians 13.

Among our friends or family we know of those who are stuck in a stage of this process. Let us not be discouraged. Our losses, our troubles, our trials, our temptations, our tribulations, our sufferings will never be more than we can withstand.

> "The temptations in your life are no different from what others experience. And God is faithful. He will not allow the temptation to be more than you can stand. When you are tempted, he will show you a way out so that you can endure" I Corinthians 10:13 NLT.

At an early stage of my studying these scriptures I discovered *Death and Dying* in which Elisabeth Kübler-Ross identified the stages of facing death as denial, anger, bargaining, depression, acceptance and hope[1]. Application of these stages has been useful in studying other losses. I am redefining the stages to integrate our physical, mental and spiritual gifts.

In this study we will challenge and encourage each other. Each of us has difficulty in dealing with one or more particular loss. Some of us get "hung up" in anger and others in sadness, etc. This approach helped many men who learned the process in weekly sessions during their rehabilitation from addiction.

---

[1] *On Death and Dying* by Elisabeth Kübler-Ross, first Touchstone Edition 1997, page 9.

It was my privilege to lead the discussion of this process in approximately 250 sessions over six years. We thoroughly discussed each stage and the men made personal applications. I particularly want to thank Mike Smith without whom I would not have had this opportunity to learn along with him as he suffered while coping with his anger and lack of hope. He agreed to write a portion of the chapter on finding meaning.

Each of us has a different set of losses over time. Our challenge is to face each loss with the expectation of being able to find meaning and adjust to that loss. The challenge is to learn to look at every loss as an opportunity to use faith, hope and love to improve ourselves as Jesus proposed when he asked us to become perfect,

> "You have heard the law that says, 'Love your neighbor' and hate your enemy. But I say, love your enemies! Pray for those who persecute you! In that way, you will be acting as true children of your Father in heaven. For He gives His sunlight to both the evil and the good, and he sends rain on the just and the unjust alike. If you love only those who love you, what reward is there for that? Even corrupt tax collectors do that much. If you are kind only to your friends, how are you different from anyone else? Even pagans do that. But you are to be perfect, even as your Father in heaven is perfect" Matthew 5:43-48 NLT.

We are on the journey to perfection and will reach our goal at redemption. Our dealing with each of our troubles using the spiritual gifts of faith, hope and love will be the engines which pull us toward perfection, to joy, even in this life.

Jesus reassured his Apostles when he said to them,
> "I have told you these things, so that in me you may have peace. In this world you will have trouble. But take heart! I have overcome the world" John 16:33 New International Version (NIV).

Thank you for beginning this book on coping with life as you experience your losses. It is my hope and expectation that you will take up the challenge. Each of us has established our individual way of dealing with losses. We can improve. That is our challenge. Take as much time as you need with each stage and restudy the chapters most difficult for you.

I

Losses

Losses will be a significant part of our lives. We have physical, mental and spiritual losses. Our human tendency is to avoid all losses at all costs. For most of us that does not work well. We will suffer losses regardless of our efforts to avoid them. We experience the grieving process each time we suffer loss. Some of us get stuck in a particular stage. Our challenge is to find the most efficient way back to joy. We seek not only to experience joy but also to improve the way we handle future losses. We can become good at reaching joy. That is our challenge.

There are as many kinds of losses and perceived losses as there are individuals. We worry about losses which never happen and we suffer unanticipated losses. Fortunately there are enough similarities in our losses to make this study together worthwhile. To find meaning in our losses is our goal and challenge.

Babies suffer from hunger and coldness of soiled diapers. Their cries solicit help but not immediate relief. Wet hungry babies suffer loss of comfort. As they learn from experience, they come to expect a new feeding and a fresh diaper. As they learn to express themselves in gestures and words, they are able to develop some patience and persistence. That is their challenge.

Preschool children learn by observing their caretakers. They imitate and try different ways of dealing with their disappointments. They spend time in imagining different situations from which they find ways of escape. The value of play is real.

School children lose the freedom of free play and the security home usually provides. They practice dealing with worst case scenario losses using imagination. Children do learn fast, but much of their success depends on repetition. They are not discouraged by failures. Jesus used the faith of children as an example of the faith we seek.

Teens often do not experience time as months or years. They think more in today or at most tomorrow. They find waiting very difficult. The powerful effects of their multiple hormones play havoc with their emotions. Teens live as if there is no death or at least not in the foreseeable future. With more freedom teens are faced with the loss of security on which they previously depended. They rebel against rules. Once they must depend on themselves, they suffer even more in developing and following their own rules. They often worry about loss of status in the eyes of their peers. They worry about how they look to others and how they compare to other teens. During sessions with teens, I was unable to adequately explain the concept of learning from their losses. They paid attention but did not apply the concept to their own experiences as did the men in rehabilitation. The teens had not yet lost everything as had the men. We do learn from our losses. Sometimes it requires repeated and severe losses.

Young adults have yet another set of losses. They have lost the security of their parents' home with hot meals and a warm, safe, dry bed. Good jobs do not come easily to most young adults so they lose the security of a routine as they had while in school. They may lose a romantic partner due to circumstances. Romantic losses are more difficult than most other losses. There is both loss of another and loss of self value in a romantic loss.

Middle-aged adults often discover a physical ailment with which they wrestle so they lose their hope of a long healthy life. They often look back and regret some of their past thoughts and actions. This may bring on depression.

Accidental injury is a major loss to which anyone has difficulty adjusting. Most of us shut down emotions and activities immediately after an accident. The toll of accidents is so great they deserve special attention. We will go into more detail in the chapter on adjusting.

If we are fortunate to live a long life, we lose physical and mental abilities. I can hardly believe that I was born in 1930. Some of my losses include unexpected blessings. My decline in memory prevents some suffering of anxiety. Each year for the last several my dermatologist has found one or more skin cancers which, if left unattended, would cause great damage. Fortunately my stroke has not recurred and my physical loss is not great. The removal of my cancerous prostate has prevented additional suffering from pain or kidney failure. My exercise stamina has not been significantly reduced by my coronary occlusion and my blood pressure is finally under control. If I live longer there will be other physical losses. If I learn to cope well with my current losses, my suffering from future losses will be less. The wisdom of being joyful with losses is finally beginning to have meaning.

As we age we may lose our perceived self-worth. Recently I discovered Ann Voskamp's *One Thousand Gifts*[2]. She describes the process of concentrating on our gifts rather than on our wishes or desires. Yes, my blessings outnumber my losses. If we keep a journal and list one blessing each day or perhaps two we will be amazed at how blessed we are. We each have a thousand or more.

Age does not guarantee an increase in our spiritual strengths. In fact, age brings more tests of our spiritual health. There are ways of suffering losses which insure improvement. Fortunately God gave us some gifts which when practiced lead to joy. Our goal is to be able to use the gifts of faith, hope and love early in our suffering. The earlier we begin the sooner we will experience joy.

Although each of us has our own particular set of losses many of us are experiencing similar losses. There is no way to live without suffering loss either now or worrying about some loss in the near future. How can we deal with the losses? One of the first methods is denial. We will study denial in the next chapter.

---

[2] *One Thousand Gifts*, Copyright © 2010 by Ann Morton Voskamp published by Zondervan.

II

Denial

Denial is the first mechanism used in dealing with loss. It may be the one most frequently used. We deny many losses, troubles, trials or the significance of them. We deny our power to adjust to the loss. We deny the importance of adjusting. We deny opportunities to adjust to losses.

Cain practiced denial as described in Genesis 4. Jehovah asked Cain where Abel was and Cain denied he knew by asking, "Am I my brother's keeper?" My greatest denial is acting as though what I eat does not cause me to be overweight. I know that it does but when sitting down to eat my denial kicks in and there is nothing left on my plate when finished. I have practiced denial to the point that I am good at it. The better I become the more I am tempted to use denial.

We deny some troubles even when obvious to others. It is known that obesity is a major factor in many diseases. I observe obese individuals in restaurants vigorously eating from an overfilled plate. They are denying their obesity is due to overeating. Even doctors have denied the importance of obesity when they fail to councel each obese patient at each visit. They and most of us anticipate failure of our efforts so we deny the opportunity to deal with this resistant problem. We often deny the significance of our other troubles.

When you tell yourself that this will be your last cigarette for the day, you are denying your addiction to nicotine. When you begin the day refusing to smoke the first cigarette and refuse each time the urge comes, then you are increasing your resistance and will eventually be able to live completely without nicotine. This principle applies to alcohol, drugs and other habits. You can use this process to deal with many troubles.

Why do we use denial so much? If I admit that overeating leads to my being overweight then I am faced with taking responsibility. If I practice denial I avoid taking responsibility. I may even deny that others see my problem. It is possible to practice denial to the point of being unable to see the truth. That is what happens when we persist in a specific sin over and over again. One can sear one's own conscience.

We are at risk of letting the devil lead us as described by James,

> "Let no man say when he is tempted, I am tempted of God; for God cannot be tempted with evil, and he himself tempteth no man: [14] but each man is tempted, when he is drawn away by his own lust, and enticed. [15] Then the lust, when it hath conceived, beareth sin: and the sin, when it is fullgrown, bringeth forth death" James 1:13-15 ASV.

Note the progression from temptation, desire, conception of pleasure, sin to death. Joe Beam, in *Seeing the Unseen*[3], thoroughly details the process from temptation to death.

Denial is not always bad. When we are dealing with several losses at the same time denial serves a useful purpose. When a man is addicted to nicotine and alcohol, it is useful to concentrate on becoming clean of alcohol and then using those acquired skills to overcome the nicotine addiction. Denial helps us function while adjusting to a loss more important or more urgent.

During my mentoring sessions at the rehab center, on several occasions I asked the members of the group how long each had lived in denial. Their answers were from a few years up to fifty. Our challenge is to move beyond denial as soon as possible.

We deny any power to change with the statement "that is just me" or "that's the way I roll." We deny that we miss opportunities to change and to improve. Some of us live in denial for years or perhaps for a lifetime. We get stuck in denial. My denial of overeating has the potential of lasting the rest of my life. Our challenge is to move out of denial. Some of the best mechanisms are faith, hope and love. We will study those in chapters 9, 10 and 11. Many of us frequently use bargaining. We will explore bargaining in the next chapter.

III

---

[3] *Seeing the Unseen* Revised © 2000 by Joe Beam, chapter 12, published by Howard Books.

Bargaining

Once we give up denial of a specific trouble we often use bargaining. We may bargain with close friends, authorities, our dependants and even God. God was very patient with Abraham when he asked that Sodom be saved for fifty righteous. After God agreed Abraham bargained with God from fifty down to forty-five, forty, thirty, twenty and finally down to ten. God agreed not to destroy Sodom if ten righteous were found. Bargaining is a good mechanism for dealing with losses. The greatest problem is if one party does not fulfill their end of the bargain as in the above example. The process of bargaining may help by making the facts clearer. Abraham was feeling for the few righteous and dared to bargain with God. God clarified His justice in destroying Sodom by permitting Abraham to bargain. Review this story in chapters 18 and 19 of Genesis.

There is currently a large movement to use bargaining, commonly called mediation or conflict resolution, with families, businesses and governmental organizations. In Tennessee we have Rule 31[4] training supervised by our Tennessee Supreme Court, where on meeting the requirements, graduates can mediate between parties in conflict over important issues. This is a very useful mechanism for dealing with conflicts. One of the incarcerated men taking college courses for whom I serve as proctor demanded so much of my time that I wrote out a contract detailing what I can do and what he can do for his education. Yes, we bargained and modified the contract until each could sign it. We now know what to expect from each other. Our bargaining has promoted peace between us.

Children learn bargaining early. Parents often introduce this mechanism by offering rewards for desired behavior. "If you finish your vegetables you may have ice cream." As they grow bargaining becomes more formal such as in paying for specific grades. Some teach bargaining by paying for chores around the house.

---

[4] Search for "tncourts.gov/rules/supreme-court/31"

Marriages work more smoothly after both agree on who will be responsible for which job. This usually requires more than one discussion, bargaining session. Bargaining, give and receive, is the course leading to an agreement. Marriages work best when the two are flexible enough to assume each other's responsibilities as needed to adjust to unplanned happenings. Most people do not realize that marriage is not just a legal contract; it is all about agreement. Bargaining is a healthy way to reach agreements.

Conferences between employees and employer are often bargaining sessions. The supervisor may seem to be the decider, but in a well-run organization, the workers are so essential their needs must be met or else the results will not reward anyone.

Bargaining with God is risky. Why? He has all the knowledge, wisdom and power. We are not on a level playing field with Him. God desires to be first. He wants us to submit to His demands. Yes, He gives us a lot of freedom desiring that we submit on our own volition. Many of our prayers are bargaining proposals to God. I do not actually say, "If you will forgive me I will improve." But, I often make a promise when I ask for his blessings. If I do this I am obligated to keep my end of the bargain. Again, we do not know what He knows so we are unable to bargain wisely. That is why we ask if it is in His will that He bless us.

In order to use bargaining wisely we should know the facts of our troubles. We need to learn our options. We are then able to prioritize our time and energy. We cannot do everything at the same time. Prioritization is necessary. Jesus explained prioritization when He said our duty is to put God first and others ahead of our self,

> "Teacher, which is the most important commandment in the Law of Moses?" Jesus replied, 'you must love the LORD your God with all your heart, all your soul, and all your mind.' This is the first and greatest commandment. A second is equally important: 'Love your neighbor as yourself.' The entire law and all the demands of the prophets are based on these two commandments" Matthew 22:36-40 NLT.

After we put God first and others ahead of ourselves we then are able to prioritize how we spend our time. When we reach the level of spiritual maturity on which we consistently place God first, then others, our bargaining is much more effective and much less harmful to ourselves and to those around us. It is likely that we react to some troubles with a higher level of maturity and to other troubles with a lower level. In using bargaining we often become angry at ourselves or others. In the next chapter we will study anger as a mechanism of dealing with losses.

IV

Anger

Have you felt the energy and motivation of anger? God built this emotion into our bodies to equip us to deal with perceived injustices. We need this emotion to give us the courage, energy and persistence to do difficult things when necessary. How can we use this God given emotion to our and other's advantage? We will explore together.

In this study we will keep our minds and hearts focused on God's will in managing anger. Jesus expressed anger. He saw the misuse of the temple courts and overturned the money changers tables (John 2:13). He was angry when He perceived the Pharisees were trying to trick Him (Mark 3:4-6). Jesus taught us that anger risks our destination (Matthew 5:21-26). What Would Jesus Do? Sometimes the answer would be turn over tables and chase people with a whip! Paul admonished us to be angry and sin not (Ephesians 4:25-27). We will strive to keep our study of anger within these principles. This will help us to modify our practice of anger to fit God's will.

There are a number of reasons we see so much anger and violence. There are more of us than ever in the same amount of space. The crowding of our highways, malls, and schools promotes conflicts. The 24/7 television and personal communication devices spread examples of how anger controls us. We instantly know of violent acts from around the world. These factors together bring anger to our attention daily. We catch that to which we are exposed. Anger is contagious.

I needed anger to motivate me to act as described next. My seeing two infants in a car in the parking lot of our local drug store with no adult in sight caused me enough anger to go in and ask that an announcement be made over the public address system describing those at-risk children. I was prepared to fight for these two infants. My risk was in causing onlookers to think that I was meddling. It certainly made the mother angry and deny that she had left them there more than a "minute."

When we display anger we run the risk of causing others to become angry. We must use our judgment whether to take that risk. I have failed to take the risk many times. I will pray more often to be wise enough to know when to intervene. I will pray to be able to be angry and sin not. What other emotion could have motivated me to intervene? Love! We will discuss love in chapter eleven.

When we see one person offend another we may need anger to motivate us. We may not be able to do anything to prevent or help but we can try. We can call attention to the injustice being done. We can empathize with the victim. We can call on others who can help.

What deserves my anger? Offenses against God should make me angry. Job was very angry with God, yet he did not sin. Job was not able to interpret God's actions correctly. We are at risk of misinterpreting others' actions. We may misinterpret and become angry at others.

Offenses against me may require anger to help me do what can be done. I may need to become angry in order to confront the offender. If I deserved to be offended then I need to adjust and learn from my mistake. In fact I may need to apologize.

When regularly angered by our intimates, we can often achieve peace by approaching them in a nonthreatening way. This usually means waiting until the current anger episode has passed. The emotion of anger often prevents our taking time to evaluate the causes of anger. That is one of the reasons this study is beneficial. Our challenge is to take the time to evaluate our choices. We can prepare for the next time we are at risk of becoming angry. This will permit us to practice "slow to anger."

If our children frequently anger us, they are also at risk. Their observations of our reaction to them will teach them to deal with their future frustrations in the same way. This can establish a generational cycle of violence.

Should we let the sun go down on our anger? No, Paul advised the Ephesians and to us to tell the truth always and not let our anger against others last overnight in order to keep the devil from tempting us (Ephesians 4:25-27.) Holding anger overnight runs the risk of planning retaliation. Harboring anger runs the risk of its becoming chronic and coming out at unexpected times. This may result in letting anger control our lives.

Can I become angry unnecessarily? The time when our youngest son and I went to our local car dealership to pick up one of our vehicles is etched in my memory. I asked for the keys after paying the bill and they responded with, "The keys are in the car." After finding the car in the rear of their unlit lot, I went back in and told everyone how displeased I was. Without using curse words, I gave them a "cursing out." On the way home I realized this was a terrible example before our sixteen-year-old son. This incident kept me from repeating the same mistake (sin) many times. I remembered James and Paul's admonition to be joyful when I meet troubles of different kinds. I could have used this incident to express my anger in a better way. The attendants probably would have learned to consider the customer first in keeping their keys secure if I had approached them with patience. Since then I have used this mistake to prevent other mistakes.

When someone I love is harmed should I become angry? Can I do otherwise? A better question is what should I do when angry? I was helped by reading and rereading Doctor Theodore Rubin's[5] *The Angry Book*. You will be helped by this book. If you are not helped enough, please ask for help from one trained and experienced in helping. After anger has lived in us for awhile, we need all of the help we can get.

---

[5] *The Angry Book* by Theodore I. Rubin, MD published by Simon & Schuster in 1997.

Suppressed anger often influences us in subtle ways. We may live with a level of anger and become accustomed to it. Chronic anger influences our blood pressure, muscle tone, gastric acid output, bowel evacuation and most other body functions. Seething anger often directs our conversation by means of criticism or abusive language to others. Suppressed anger risks sudden unexpected outbursts such as road rage or injury to individuals.

The combination of suppressed anger and resentment results in planned mass injury. There are many less glaring expressions of anger seen as abuse in families and the workplace. These more private expressions are often devastating to those involved.

Paul advised us,
> "Therefore, putting away lying, let every man speak truth with his brother, for we are members one of another. Be angry, and sin not: let not the sun go down on your wrath, neither give place to the devil" Ephesians 4:25-27, 21st Century King James Version (KJ21).

The challenge of dealing with today's anger today while "sinning not" has been a challenge to most of us. My tendency has been to suppress my anger. That is risky.

As we move from anger in dealing with our losses, we find blaming equally as challenging in the next chapter.

V

Blaming

Who is to blame for my troubles? Several years ago a study of the surviving parents of a large group of leukemic children revealed that most blamed someone. Approximately half blamed themselves for their child's death. The others blamed someone such as their doctors, God, etc.

Self-blame is frequent and sometimes it is appropriate. I am totally to blame for my being overweight. It is not my hormones. It is the mathematics of intake minus energy expended. Self-blame is convenient and easy. But if self blame is practiced frequently it robs one of confidence and enthusiasm. It is not always possible to accurately access the true blame especially where there is a series of failures.

I did case reviews of medical malpractice cases and learned about meta-analysis used in studying medical mistakes where one can identify specific causes such as inaccurate patient identification, illegible handwriting or a failure to follow a proven treatment process. We have an opportunity to learn from our own failures in order to prevent them in the future. In the spiritual realm God gave us recommendations based on the fact that we will have failures. He also told us what to do about them.

Jesus admonishes us to,

> "Ye therefore shall be perfect, as your heavenly Father is perfect" Matt. 5:48 ASV.

Later John explains,

> "If we claim to be without sin, we deceive ourselves and the truth is not in us. [9] If we confess our sins, he is faithful and just and will forgive us our sins and purify us from all unrighteousness. [10] If we claim we have not sinned, we make Him out to be a liar and His word is not in us" I John 1:8-10 New International Version (NIV).

We are not perfect, but we are on the way and we will reach perfection in heaven. During our repentance of sin, we can analyze the process of our having gone from temptation, to desire, to conceiving pleasure, to sin and into death so that we can develop resistance to sin. Norman Vincent Peale described how he avoided lust (temptation, desire, conceiving pleasure) by praying for the beautifully attractive women he saw. This prevented his sinning.

In our rehab sessions, the men would either blame themselves or find others to blame for their continuing in addiction. When a man consistently blamed others, we soon realized this was his mechanism for dealing with his loss and not likely the true cause.

In most losses there are multiple failures where blame could be assigned. Some of the blame is ours and sometimes others are to blame. Sometimes we never know who is to blame. Job did not likely learn during his lifetime what caused his suffering.

As we move through blaming, let us strive to find joy in our troubles. On our way toward looking for joy, we will next visit sadness.

VI

Sadness/Depression

Sadness is a normal part of dealing with loss or the fear of loss. In sadness we slow down and reflect on the causes of the sadness. Did someone fail us? Did we fail them? Did we fail ourselves? This self analysis is a painful part of sadness. We may, in the depth of sadness, lose hope for the future and become depressed. Loss of hope is a central element of depression.

During this time of self-reflecting, we have the opportunity to correct our course or to confront those who failed us. We will not likely have these opportunities unless we suffer sadness. God gives us the opportunity to reflect on the past. A problem is that sadness saps us of any enthusiasm to do this hard work. We all have the opportunity to encourage and build up those in sadness.

Some of us go directly to sadness, skipping denial, blaming and anger. Our hereditary and our experiences may lead us from loss to sadness or even into depression. Others seem to feel enthusiastic in face of all circumstances. This chapter will not go deeply into the psychological or medical aspects of depression but will focus on our developing spiritual strengths which help us in managing our sadness and depression.

The book of Job is a place to learn about sadness/depression. I have wondered if Job now realizes how important his life was for many of us who have studied his story. We may not realize how suffering through our current loss will benefit us. It certainly benefited the Christians living in the Roman Empire as described in Revelation. Chapter 6 and 7 describe the heavenly scene where the dead martyrs were in front of the throne. Most of us will not experience death by persecution, but any current suffering prepares us for future suffering as necessary. Remember, our goal is to be joyful when we suffer losses of many kinds. We need not seek suffering. It will come. It is our challenge to suffer in a way that increases our patience, endurance and hope.

Clinical depression differs from sadness in that it is more severe. The number of losses, our heredity and our past experiences all contribute to our risk of developing clinical depression. Each of us has a different combination of factors. It cannot be mathematically explained. There is a decline from sadness into clinical depression.

Clinical depression is a serious medical illness. It's more than just feeling "down in the dumps" or "blue" for a few days. It is feeling down or low and hopeless for weeks at a time.

Signs and symptoms of depression are detailed in the NIH[6] web page:

- Persistent sad, anxious, or "empty" feelings
- Feelings of hopelessness or pessimism
- Feelings of guilt, worthlessness, or helplessness
- Irritability, restlessness
- Loss of interest in activities or hobbies once pleasurable including sex
- Fatigue and decreased energy
- Difficulty concentrating, remembering details, and making decisions
- Insomnia, early-morning wakefulness, or excess sleeping
- Overeating, or appetite loss
- Thoughts of suicide, suicide attempts
- Aches or pains, headaches, cramps, or digestive problems that do not ease even with treatment.

This web source is updated periodically and documents the standard of care at the time.

Depression robs one of enthusiasm. The word "en-thus-iasm" was derived from "God inspired". We are the physical manifestation of God in that He lives in us as the Holy Spirit. This study is for the purpose of developing the ability to let His Spirit rule our lives and drive out fear or depression. He will forgive us for any failures in our past if only we ask and repent as prescribed by Peter,

---

[6] www.nimh.nih.gov   Go to Depression/Signs & Symptoms

"So let everyone in Israel know for certain that God has made this Jesus, whom you crucified, to be both Lord and Messiah!" Peter's words pierced their hearts, and they said to him and to the other apostles, 'Brothers, what should we do?' Peter replied, 'Each of you must repent of your sins and turn to God, and be baptized in the name of Jesus Christ for the forgiveness of your sins. Then you will receive the gift of the Holy Spirit. This promise is to you, and to your children, and even to the Gentiles—all who have been called by the Lord our God.' Then Peter continued preaching for a long time, strongly urging all his listeners, 'Save yourselves from this crooked generation.' Those who believed what Peter said were baptized and added to the church that day— about 3,000 in all" Acts 2:36-41 NLT.

God has given us many ways of dealing with depression. Exercise is the most effective, available, economical and safest treatment of depression. In fact exercise has a firm physiological basis. Exercise releases hormones which elevate our mood. One of these hormones is beta-endorphin which is released into the blood stream from the pituitary gland.

One of the reasons sadness is so prevalent is that most of us do little exercise. Our work is done by machines. The bricks I used to unload from a box car in a few days are now unloaded by one man operating a fork lift in a few hours. Other effective antidepressants are adequate sleep, adequate fluid intake and a balanced diet.

Clinical depression should not cause the victim to feel guilty. We should always be inclined to offer relief by known methods of treatment including the use of drugs. There are myths about drug treatment of depression. Since some depression is precipitated by the use of street drugs there is a myth that the depressed person should not use effective drugs to help their depression. That is untrue. The myth that all drugs are addicting is not true. The myth that spiritual adjustments are the only things needed in treating depression is untrue.

There are now more than twenty drugs used to treat depression. Although there are known qualities about each drug, no one is able to predict accurately which drug should be used first in a specific person. There are known qualities about many drugs allowing accurate predictions that some specific drugs should not be used in a specific person. If a drug is known to cause overeating it should not be used in an obese person. When the drugs being used are not resulting in improvement after a few weeks, the patient should ask for a consultation on drug therapy.

The full effect of the starting dose of a drug requires from 4 to 6 weeks. This is a big disadvantage. Since the side effects of a full dose may be too much for the patient to tolerate one must begin with small doses and work up. To achieve the optimum doses of the optimum combination of medications may take a few months, so there is a danger the patient will give up on drug treatments.

There is a great variation in the cost of drugs. If a drug has been around long enough to be on the generic list they are much less expensive. The side effects and effectiveness of generic drugs are also better known. Newer drugs may not have been used in enough patients to learn all of their undesired side effects. Some side effects are desirable. If a patient is underweight, a drug with overeating as a side effect is desirable. If a patient has promiscuity as a symptom, a drug which decreases libido may be helpful.

Our exercising, sleeping adequate amounts, eating well, using our gifts of faith, hope and love, thanking God for these gifts and asking God for the ability to overcome depression may not be enough. God also gave us psychotherapists and antidepressant drugs for our benefit.

As we move beyond sadness we will work on adjusting to our losses in the next chapter.

VII

Adjusting

As we moved through the previous stages, we were attempting to adjust by denying, bargaining, becoming angry, blaming and feeling depressed. There is the possibility of getting stuck in any one of these stages. We may have stayed in a specific stage for some time but when we move to adjusting we will be climbing up the positive side of the clock toward joy. The great spiritual gifts of faith, hope and love will be the engines pulling us to joy.

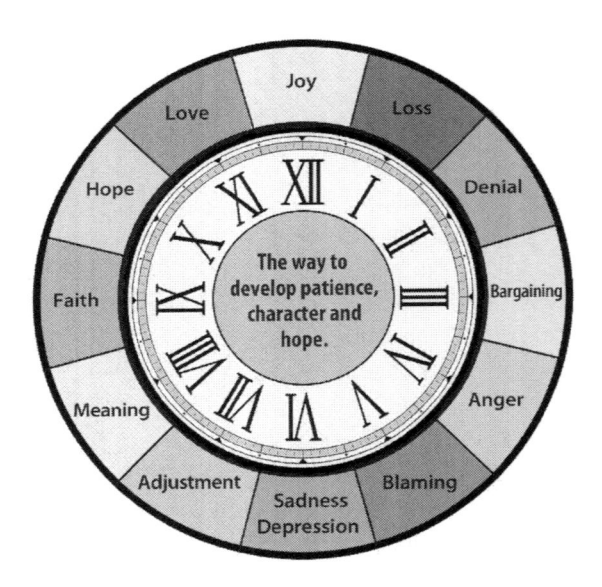

Adjusting is more than accepting. Adjusting to a loss includes recognizing the loss as significant and seeking the best remedy for that loss. That may include doing without or substituting something to take its place. Often we are unable to say "I am extremely joyful that I have experienced this loss." Later after we find meaning in the loss we may be able to be joyful.

Most adjustments do not come automatically, but they require planning, hard work and prayer for God's help. Some of the hard work is being thankful for those blessings we have remaining.

Paul advised that we,
> "Rejoice in the Lord always. I will say it again: Rejoice! Let your gentleness be evident to all. The Lord is near. Do not be anxious about anything, but in everything by prayer and petition, with thanksgiving, present your requests to God. And the peace of God, which transcends all understanding, will guard your hearts and your minds in Christ Jesus" Philippians 4:4-7 NIV.

Most of us remember this scripture when we are joyful, but it also applies when we are depressed and attempting to adjust to a loss.

The loss of a body function is a particularly difficult adjustment. One's whole life is changed. One's body image is changed forever. Accidents resulting in the loss of limbs, etc., are most difficult since there is no time for preparation. This will cause and actually require a period of sadness/depression before any adjustment can occur. There are many possible accidental losses of important bodily parts, thus specific preparation is impossible.

Remember God's assurance when suffering,
> "We can rejoice, too, when we run into problems and trials, for we know that they help us develop endurance. And endurance develops strength of character, and character strengthens our confident hope of salvation. And this hope will not lead to disappointment. For we know how dearly God loves us, because he has given us the Holy Spirit to fill our hearts with his love" Romans 5:3-5 NLT.

When the loss is of something for which there is hope in replacing we can progress faster. That is true of most of our possessions. You who have lost fortunes can have hope of regaining sufficient wealth on which to live.

My adjustment to a stroke at the age of 70 was relatively easy since I lost only the sensation of touch on my right side. My father's stroke was a more severe loss at the age of 49 since he was paralyzed on his left side until his death at age 89. He adjusted successfully by driving a truck from which he sold tools to auto mechanics.

Losing a loved one in death is usually the most difficult loss we suffer. Our memories help us to adjust. We remember emotional events best. We remember pleasant emotions better than unpleasant ones. If we have the hope of seeing them in eternity the loss is much less but still present. We must suffer some in sadness and perhaps depression. When a loved one dies after months of suffering we are much better prepared by their suffering.

We will work on finding meaning in our losses in the next chapter.

VIII

Meaning

If we find the meaning in a loss early on we are fortunate. Often this is not the case. Finding meaning may require the rest of our life. We may have to wait until eternity to know why we had to suffer some losses. We may never know.

We have no information on whether Job knew that God had permitted Satan to test him to prove his faithfulness.

We know,
> "Then Job replied to the Lord: "I know that you can do all things; no plan of yours can be thwarted. You asked, 'Who is this that obscures my counsel without knowledge?' Surely I spoke of things I did not understand, things too wonderful for me to know. "You said, 'Listen now, and I will speak; I will question you, and you shall answer me.' My ears had heard of you but now my eyes have seen you. Therefore I despise myself and repent in dust and ashes" Job 42:1-6 NIV.

Job found meaning to his losses in that he was able to pray for the repentance of his friends who offended God in their explanations of Him. He found meaning in that he was rewarded with ten more children and more possessions than before.

Our injured soldiers often express the meaning of their loss of limbs or other body functions as the preservation of our freedom. Their relatives describe the meaning of their loved ones having lost their lives as defending our lives. They have found meaning at a great cost. The veterans who have lost so much often express thanks for what they have left of family and their opportunity to be of service to others. One of the most effective ways to find meaning is to be thankful for what we still have.

While growing up, I had a dream of being a pilot. I lived close to Trade-A-Plane in Crossville, TN, and I wanted desperately to work there to be close to flying. As it was never possible, I lost that opportunity. Years later, after being happy in the practice of pediatrics, I found meaning to that previous loss of opportunity. If I had become a pilot, I would have missed the many times I was needed in helping families through their losses. When we look back on losses, we often can see how it worked out best for us and others.

Mike Smith, my brother in Christ referenced in the introduction chapter, will next describe his finding meaning and purpose in his significant losses.

My Purpose

I want to share my pain and how I found purpose in the darkness. I was sitting in a cold jail cell in 2006. I was scared, beat up and dead inside. In my heart there was no God, and in my mind I had nothing to offer him anyway. I remember sitting on my bed and a guy from the next cell asked me if I had anything to read, and I responded, "No". Through a crack in the corner of the cell, he gave me a small New Testament Bible. I had nothing else going on, so I decided to make the most of my time and give it a try.

I began reading the Gospel of Matthew. For the first time in my life, I read about Jesus. Sure, I knew who He was but I had never known what He went through. After I read Matthew, I read Mark, and then I came to the book of Luke. I think it was in that book that things came into focus for me. I read the parable of the prodigal son. As I read through the parable it became clear what the message said to me. No matter what I did, God was always standing at the road waiting for me with his arms extended. I was so confused and I asked myself what did Jesus want with me?

I continued reading. I learned the sacrifice that He made for the world and a sinner like me. I don't think I have ever felt so low in my life. I began reading Acts and read about Paul. Paul was a worse sinner than I was. The grace that was extended to him by Jesus and the purpose that lay ahead of Paul drove me to think that perhaps I, too, had purpose and just had to find it.

I needed encouragement, I needed guidance and I needed to know where to begin. I received a complete Bible and began reading it in my search. I came to the book of Job. I was amazed at the amount of punishment one man (other than Jesus) could take and remain faithful.

From Job 1:20-22,
> "Then Job arose, and rent his mantle, and shaved his head, and fell down upon the ground, and worshipped, And said, Naked came I out of my mother's womb, and naked shall I return thither: the Lord gave, and the Lord hath taken away; blessed be the name of the Lord. In all this Job sinned not, nor charged God foolishly" King James Version.

At this point I was not even out of the first chapter, and I could relate so much to Job. I felt his pain, anguish and the anger that he felt and confusion that must have been within him. I was nowhere as faithful as he, but I felt our losses were comparable. We both lost our families and felt abandoned by God in our time of need. I knew then what needed to be done. I found myself the same way as Job-- naked and with nothing left to lose. I hit my knees in that cell and cried out to Jesus to save my soul and come into my heart. I awoke the next day with a hunger for the word of God. Through the book of Jonah I realized that perhaps God had been reaching for me all along, and this cell that held me was the great fish which swallowed me whole so that it would be God and me alone. I was baptized in August of 2006. I did not know what to expect. Going in with all the hurt, anger and hatred I felt for those who hurt me, I was not looking at it the other way around. As I was dipped the water was cold, suffocating, but as I came out I felt something different. It was as if the weight of the world had instantly been lifted from me. I had come out of the darkness and into the light. That experience is something I can never forget. I pledged to God to give him everything of me and I knew through his word he would create something out of me. I knew in order to move forward I would have to remove all the things that made me the person I then was.

I decided to give God the biggest things of all, my hatred and anger. I had a stepfather who physically and mentally abused me from age 5 until I was 13. When my mother decided to leave him, I held on to the biggest grudge I had ever held. I vowed to myself that I would get bigger, stronger and come back to take my revenge on him. My whole life revolved around that experience. It was my way of taking the focus off my own actions. In view of the steps I had recently taken I knew my next step would make or break me. I told God I did not want to be angry or hate anyone anymore. I did not want to carry this burden I had carried for so long and I asked God to take it from me. I did not expect it to be instant or for some miraculous beam of light to come down on me.

The next morning I awoke and for the first time since I was a young child; I was not angry anymore. The place in my heart where I let my anger and hatred lie was not there anymore. I knew then that everything happening was for a bigger purpose in my life.

It is hard to find purpose while living in the dark. Most people are consumed with anger and resentment and that combination makes it hard to allow anything else in your heart. I believe that at your most vulnerable point in your life is where God stands at that road and waits for you to return. Looking back now on my life, if anyone had told me I'd be where I am today I would have laughed at them. I knew once I gave my life to God and asked Him to live in my heart that He would never let me go again.

Once I completed my jail sentence, I entered a rehab facility where I got involved in a church, but knew nothing about how to live the Christian life. I became cocky and arrogant, and I allowed what I did know to be used for reasons other than were intended. I learned a great lesson from my arrogance. I went through a four-month rehab, and on the last day, the day of graduation, I had relapsed but denied it, made excuses, and left thinking I had all I needed.

I had a friend who had been there for me and who helped through all my ordeals while being locked up, and he got me into an apartment of my own. I had also enrolled into college. I knew what purpose God had in store for me, but I still wanted to hold on to my addiction and my own selfish desires. I used the money I had gotten in student loans and began using drugs full time. I was working in a local restaurant to support myself, but that only prolonged my time using drugs.

My probation officer knew I was still using, and I was in danger of being sent back to jail. From there I would have to go to prison and serve the rest of my time. She informed me that I would need to get into some sort of inpatient rehab or I would be violating probation. By this time, the money was running out. I had started using my family and friends again, and I was stealing from them in order to feed my addiction. The rent I had paid was running out, and so was my drug money. As I sat in my living room, I was searching on the Internet for a program that would satisfy my probation officer. I discovered The Mission in Nashville. Concurrently, my probation officer found the same one.

God works in ways I was never meant to understand. I believe He used my probation officer and me to come across the life recovery program together. By the time I returned to her office and explained it, she had already gotten me admitted. Through all the darkness of my life, I never doubted that God had left me. I knew it would all be used for His glory and His purpose. I guess I knew what was expected of me, but I was scared to face my own destiny and move on to it. I wanted the perks but I did not want to do any of the work to get there. God has a way of showing us the path which we are to take. Though we may stray, it seems always to circle back and allows us to use the experience to be effective in God's Kingdom.

Going into the Rescue Mission, I never knew what to expect from it. As I walked through the gates, I saw a sea of homeless people walking around. I had never before in my life seen a homeless person, and at that time I never wanted to see one again. I returned and sat in my car for about an hour struggling with going home, but the thought of being locked up again was burning through my head.

I finally brought myself to go back in and see what I had gotten myself into. My first hour there, I was scared to death. I didn't know what I was doing. I was surrounded by 24 people in a room, and we had to share a shower with the homeless. I was mortified. In my mind I was better than these people and deserved better. It was there that God really got hold of my heart. The first night, they had a chapel service. At the end, they asked if anyone wanted to receive or rededicate his life to Christ. At that moment, I felt the Lord pulling me, but I resisted. I told myself if it happened for three straight times, I would know God was speaking directly to me.

On the third night, when the altar call was given, I stood up and instantly I was taken back to a time that I felt God move through me. It was at a teen church camp. It was the first time I was asked to share my story. I was so nervous; I didn't know where to begin. As I spoke, I remember how it began to come to me, and as many times as I tripped over my words, I felt good about being able to confess to around 100 people my wrongs and how I allowed God to come into my life. When I finished, every one of those kids came and laid hands on me and prayed for me. I had never had that happen to me before, but I felt more alive than I ever had in my life. I knew then what my purpose was.

I told Jesus in that Mission chapel that I was willing, and asked Him to save me again because I knew I would die. I had hit rock bottom, and there was nowhere else to go but up. Author Dean Koontz said, "Because God is never cruel; there is a reason for all things. We must know the pain of loss; because if we never knew it, we would have no compassion for others, and we would become monsters of self-regard, creatures of unalloyed self-interest. The terrible pain of loss teaches humility to our prideful kind, has the power to soften uncaring hearts, to make a better person of a good one."

God certainly has a way of showing you how you can be what some consider the worst of the worst, and yet God will still raise you up to lead others. The program I was in was basically a Bible boot camp. I was convinced that God had all this planned just for me. With no outside distractions to lure me away, disowned by family, it was just God and me. God opened my eyes to his word and spoke to my heart. As I began reading through His word, I came upon a verse in the book of Ezekiel. It said that "a new heart also will I give you, and a new spirit will I put within you: and I will take away the stony heart out of your flesh, and I will give you a heart of flesh. And I will put My spirit within you, and cause you to walk in my statutes, and ye shall keep my judgments, and do them." I felt that God was telling me that I didn't have to live in my addiction forever. I hit my knees in my room and asked God to take away my addiction; I felt more need to rid myself of that chain that held me in sin. I can describe this experience as God giving me a new heart and taking out the heart of addiction. All the holes where I worshipped drugs, money, belongings, and anything else that was not God-God put his Spirit within those holes and filled me up.

After finishing the program I began to work in the education department of The Rescue Mission. I was working closely with the men I had been with in the program. A new sense of wants and needs filled my soul as I began. I was no scholar in high school but God showed me I was smarter than I thought. Two weeks after I began working at the Mission I enrolled in school. It was online, and I thought it would serve me best rather than going to classes where I felt inadequate compared to the younger people in the class. I was planning to major in psychology. I knew that was where I needed to be.

About one and a half years into school and work, I was given the opportunity to counsel men in the program. My passion raced as I began to help others as I had been helped to come to the Lord, to lean on Him in my time of need. Through my education, I learned a variety of lessons about human behavior and addictive behaviors that aided me while I worked with these men. In my mind and my heart I was fulfilling my purpose in God. I had given up my addiction and now I could share those experiences to help others.

Max Lucado said that God uses our pain to bring peace within us. I never understood that until I began writing this, my story. Through the suffering, pain and darkness that was my life I discovered purpose. From all I have gone through, I think I learned some very powerful lessons. I have been blessed to teach others and to allow them to make the decision for themselves. Yet God also wants us to realize there are consequences to our decisions and actions. Some of us need a bigger spiritual paddle on the rear-end from God. We <u>think</u> we know the condition of our heart, but God tells us in His

Word that we really don't. Realizing your purpose and living your purpose are two completely different things. We may realize our own potential and know deep down what God has in store for our lives. We know how we can serve God in the way He intended, but if we fail to follow through with what God has planned for us and use God's gifts for our own wants and needs then we will suffer God's consequences. The realization is that through living God's purpose for you, God will bless you in return. I lived in the halfway house at the Mission for 8 months. I was truly living God's purpose, and because I remained faithful to God He blessed me with everything I asked for in my life. I was given a wife, children and a good job serving the Lord. Everything the devil had taken from me was restored.

Today, I continue to serve God. The Lord showed me I was still teachable and showed me how to sharpen my skills for the purpose I was given. I have been in school since 2008, and in early 2014 will graduate from college with a master's degree in psychology. The past five years have taught me how to better understand men and their sin and why they do the things they do. Compassion has allowed me to see hurt that comes to everyone in a variety of ways. God has shined a light through me to those hurting and needing help that I may show them through my example how to regain their life from any life-controlling addictions and disabilities.

To sum this up, I have learned that the heart is where natural God-given emotions reside. To have one's heart taken away is to take away the desire for the natural things that God has given us: such as family, healthy relationships, good work, and moral ethics. Paul was someone whose calling fantastically matched his abilities, personality and a number of other important factors. My story illustrates that.

So, if you feel that God is not answering your prayers for direction, it is possible that God will speak to you through the process of your gaining a better understanding of who you are and what you have to offer. It took my living in a small jail cell surrounded by people whom society called "undesirable" for me to learn compassion for others and to allow me to see what I have to offer.

I was told once that when we feel we have no purpose, we essentially feel useless. Purpose and vision are interwoven essentials to carrying out the call God has for each of our lives. Without vision and purpose we cannot move forward into the new dreams and blessings God has for us.

Thank you Mike.
You have given meaning to my struggle with the troubles presented in visiting with and corresponding with men and women in jail.
Harold

IX

Faith

When I have faith in you I believe and trust you to do what you said or led me to believe. When you fail me I still have faith in you but if you repeatedly fail me I will lose faith. Open your favorite translation and check the following evidences paraphrased from chapter 11 of Hebrews.

Faith is the assurance that things we are working for will come to pass (Hebrews 11:1-2).

Our understanding how God spoke the worlds into existence out of nothing comes by faith and not by science (11:3).

Abel still speaks to us about righteousness through obedience in his offerings (11:4). Enoch bypassed death by being well pleasing to God (11:5). These accounts of Abel and Enoch are two specific examples of great personal faith.

The essence of faith is that God rewards our belief in Him and is not pleased unless we do believe (11:6).

By faith Noah did things that seemed insane to those around him. He built an ark on dry land without any reason other than that God told him to do it. This was God's way of condemning the unrighteousness of those living around Noah (11:7).

Abraham by faith left his home without specific instructions and lived in tents with his wife and sons looking for the city built by God. Abraham did his part in God's plan by faith without ever seeing the results (11:8-10).

Sarah and Abraham were past the age of childbearing but had faith that God's promise to them would result in offspring too numerous to be counted (11:11-12).

God is faithful even though our earthly life will not be long enough to see the full results of our obedience to His commands. We will not see Heaven while here but will look forward until we die because we believe Him. God is not ashamed of us and has prepared a city for us (11:13-16).

When God told Abraham to sacrifice his only promised son, Isaac, he raised his hand to slay Isaac because he knew God had a reason and a solution to these contradictory commands (11:17-19). Can you imagine killing your only promised son as a sacrifice to God? That must be the reason we call Abraham the father of the faithful. He passed his faith to his children and their children (11:20-21).

Our waiting on promises and hopes requires faith and also generates more faith in our descendants. When Joseph was sold into slavery and when he was falsely charged of rape and thrown into jail and even when he died he had not seen the results of his suffering. He was in God's great plan for the children of Israel to produce our saviour Jesus Christ. Joseph is a witness for us to make it easier for us to believe God's promise to us (11:22). If we put God first and think of our neighbors second, He will put our needs first so we do not need to be concerned. What a promise! We are tempted to concentrate on our losses and go into depression after practicing denial, blaming and anger.

Moses' parents had faith to hide him in the river in denying the king's commandment. Moses had faith enough to leave Egypt when in trouble. He had faith enough to go back to Egypt at God's command to lead the children of Israel out of Egypt. They crossed the Red sea with a wall of water threatening them (11:23-29). Can you imagine the faith it took for them to walk beside a wall of water ready to drown them as it did the Egyptians after the Israelites had crossed?

By faith the soldiers marched around the walls of Jericho for seven days because God told them to do it. Rahab had faith enough to let the spies of God down to safety and was rewarded for doing so (11:30-31).

There were so many more with great faith that the Hebrew writer did not have time to list them all but listed: Gideon, Barak, Samson, Jephthah, David and Samuel who did very difficult things by faith (11:32-34).

Faith was the power by which great and otherwise impossible things were done. Our faith in God will make it possible to do things that are impossible for us. This will occur only if we are doing what God has in His plan. Our challenge is to listen to Him as He reveals His plan for us through His word and through His Spirit.

God expects us to work within His plan. We are his hands and feet and mouth for those who do not know Him. James speaks to this,

> " So you see, faith by itself isn't enough. Unless it produces good deeds, it is dead and useless. [18] Now someone may argue, "Some people have faith; others have good deeds." But I say, "How can you show me your faith if you don't have good deeds? I will show you my faith by my good deeds."[19] You say you have faith, for you believe that there is one God. Good for you! Even the demons believe this, and they tremble in terror" James 2:17-19 NLT.

We make mistakes in our faith. We sometimes do not understand the person or system we trust. In this way we have a false faith. It is our lack of knowledge that contributes to this lack of faith. Example: As I was writing this, I received on my iPad a message offering me 1,000,000.00 US dollars if I would send 150.00 dollars by wire to an attorney in Benue Republic. This attempted scam is frequently seen. This would be a false faith to believe.

It is our responsibility to know the reason for our faith. Faith in another person or a system comes from their history. We have examples of this concept in scripture such as follows,

> "[11] As Scripture says, 'Anyone who believes in Him will never be put to shame.' [12] For there is no difference between Jew and Gentile—the same Lord is Lord of all and richly blesses all who call on him, [13] for, 'Everyone who calls on the name of the Lord will be saved.' [14] How, then, can they call on the one they have not believed in? And how can they believe in the one of whom they have not heard? And how can they hear without someone preaching to them? [15] And how can anyone preach unless they are sent? As it is written: 'How beautiful are the feet of

> those who bring good news!' ¹⁶ But not all the Israelites accepted the good news. For Isaiah says, 'Lord, who has believed our message?'¹⁷ Consequently, faith comes from hearing the message, and the message is heard through the word about Christ" Romans 10:11-17 NIV.

Faith comes from hearing the good news from a reliable source.

Faith and hope are very close as you will see as we study hope in the next chapter.

> "Being therefore justified by faith, we have peace with God through our Lord Jesus Christ; ² through whom also we have had our access by faith into this grace wherein we stand; and we rejoice in <u>hope</u> of the glory of God" Romans 5:1-2 ASV.

X

Hope

In conversation, we use the word "hope" loosely. I hope my team wins. I hope to win the lottery. I hope you have a good time. The Merriman-Webster Dictionary defines hope as "to cherish a desire with anticipation, to desire with expectation of obtainment." As we use hope loosely, we are wishing but not planning to do anything about achieving our wish. In this chapter we will use hope in the dictionary and biblical sense.

What are your hopes? Love, money, helping others, recognition, sports stardom, etc., are frequently our hopes. You and I have held some of these hopes. In my junior year of high school, I began to hope to become a doctor. I knew a surgeon who was happy and who was helping others daily. I began to inquire what I should do to become a physician. I learned that Latin was a prerequisite. Even though I did not enjoy or appreciate it, I took two years of Latin under a difficult teacher. Medical school was difficult. It was difficult for me to be joyful when faced with a hard course or a difficult instructor. As it turned out, that was the way to develop the patience and persistence to serve difficult families in practice. I was not yet spiritually mature enough to be joyful in all of my suffering.

For brief periods of time, I have hoped to win the Mega Millions lottery. After reading an article on the mathematical possibility of my winning, I gave up buying lottery tickets. In fact, statistics show there is little hope of winning the lottery.

How do we come to hope for something? We hear about it or see it in others. We read about the object of our hope. We use historical knowledge to build our hope in business, sports and entertainment. Paul suggested the same,
> "For everything that was written in the past was written to teach us, so that through endurance taught in the Scriptures and the encouragement they provide we might have hope" Romans 15:4 NIV.

This applies to our physical, mental and spiritual life.

Some combinations of hopes are incompatible. If I hope for wealth, leisure, pleasure, and security, I will find that planning for and achieving all of them will be impossible. We must integrate our hopes in order to insure success.

We have struggles in life but with great hope as explained by Paul,

> "[20] Against its will, all creation was subjected to God's curse. But with eager hope, [21] the creation looks forward to the day when it will join God's children in glorious freedom from death and decay. [22] For we know that all creation has been groaning as in the pains of childbirth right up to the present time. [23] And we believers also groan, even though we have the Holy Spirit within us as a foretaste of future glory, for we long for our bodies to be released from sin and suffering. We, too, wait with eager hope for the day when God will give us our full rights as His adopted children, including the new bodies He has promised us. [24] We were given this hope when we were saved. (If we already have something, we don't need to hope for it. [25] But if we look forward to something we don't yet have, we must wait patiently and confidently.) [26] And the Holy Spirit helps us in our weakness. For example, we don't know what God wants us to pray for. But the Holy Spirit prays for us with groanings that cannot be expressed in words" Romans 8:20-26 NLT.

What do I hope for at the end of my life? Paul answers,

> "¹¹ As Scripture says, 'Anyone who believes in Him will never be put to shame.' ¹² For there is no difference between Jew and Gentile—the same Lord is Lord of all and richly blesses all who call on Him, ¹³ for, 'Everyone who calls on the name of the Lord will be saved'" Romans 10:11-13 ASV.

How did I develop that hope? The combination of reading and hearing the scriptures on how God dealt with people in the past, plus the evidence in lives of people who have suffered great losses yet are now living well, has been all the evidence I need. I am reassured by God's words that He loves me as discussed in the next chapter.

XI

Love

Since love is the greatest of our spiritual gifts we should understand it and use it to the fullest. God through men described three kinds of love. Eros is the sum of our instincts for self-preservation. Phileo is the love we have for our fellow humans. Agape is the aspect of love qualifying it as the greatest of our spiritual gifts (I Cor. 13:13).

Eros

Without eros, we would not be here. The desire to replenish our strength by eating makes us go out and hunt and gather. The desire to defend ourselves gives us the courage to flee or fight. The desire to preserve our kind makes us pursue a sexual partner and go through all of the complexity of a sexual union. These desires are strong and pleasurable. We will not try to discuss eros fully. Amazon has over 10,000 books listed under eros. The Apostle Paul commented on eros,

> "[12] 'All things are lawful unto me,' but all things are not expedient. 'All things are lawful for me,' but I will not be brought under the power of any. [13] 'Meats for the belly, and the belly for meats,' but God shall destroy both it and them. Now the body is not for fornication, but for the Lord; and the Lord for the body. [14] And God hath both raised up the Lord and will also raise up us by His own power. [15] Know ye not that your bodies are the members of Christ? Shall I then take the members of Christ and make them the members of a harlot? God forbid! [16] What? Know ye not that he who is joined to a harlot is one body with her? 'For two,' saith He, 'shall be one flesh.' [17] But he that is joined unto the Lord is one spirit. [18] Flee fornication. Every other sin which a man doeth is outside the body, but he that committeth fornication sinneth against his own body. [19] What? Know ye not

that your body is the temple of the Holy Ghost which is in you and which ye have from God, and that ye are not your own? [20] For ye are bought with a price. Therefore glorify God in your body and in your spirit, which are God's" I Corinthians 6 KJ21.

Paul could have married, but he chose not to for his own reasons. Here he is teaching us to respect our bodies and use our God given erotic emotions in a way that keeps our bodies for the higher purpose of holding God's Holy Spirit.

Phileo

The brotherly love termed phileo is the love which builds relationships in family, community or church. We love those like us or with whom we share space and troubles. This is the love we use to help maintain peace. We have an early example of phileo,

> "And it came to pass, when he had made an end of speaking unto Saul, that the soul of Jonathan was knit with the soul of David, and Jonathan loved him as his own soul. [2] And Saul took him that day, and would let him go no more home to his father's house. [3] Then Jonathan and David made a covenant, because he loved him as his own soul. [4] And Jonathan stripped himself of the robe that was upon him, and gave it to David, and his apparel, even to his sword, and to his bow, and to his girdle" I Samuel 18:1-4 ASV.

Paul wrote to the Romans on how to practice phileo,

> "[13] Share with the Lord's people who are in need. Practice hospitality. [14] Bless those who persecute you; bless and do not curse.[15] Rejoice with those who rejoice; mourn with those who mourn.[16] Live in harmony with one another. Do not be proud, but be willing to associate with people of low position. Do not be conceited. [17] Do not repay anyone evil for evil. Be careful to do what is right in the eyes of everyone.[18] If it is possible, as far as it

depends on you, live at peace with everyone" Romans 12:13-18 NIV.

Agape

In following Jesus we will merge the three forms of love (eros, phileo and agape) into our working relationships with individuals, spiritual siblings and with God. Without this love we are without hope. Paul speaks to this gift of love,

> "If I speak with human eloquence and angelic ecstasy but don't love, I'm nothing but the creaking of a rusty gate. ² If I speak God's Word with power, revealing all His mysteries and making everything plain as day, and if I have faith that says to a mountain, 'Jump' and it jumps, but I don't love, I'm nothing. ³⁻⁷ If I give everything I own to the poor and even go to the stake to be burned as a martyr, but I don't love, I've gotten nowhere. So, no matter what I say, what I believe, and what I do, I'm bankrupt without love. Love never gives up. Love cares more for others than for self. Love doesn't want what it doesn't have. Love doesn't strut, Doesn't have a swelled head, Doesn't force itself on others, Isn't always 'me first.' Doesn't fly off the handle, Doesn't keep score of the sins of others, Doesn't revel when others grovel, Takes pleasure in the flowering of truth, Puts up with anything, Trusts God always, Always looks for the best, Never looks back, But keeps going to the end. ⁸⁻¹⁰ Love never dies. Inspired speech will be over some day; praying in tongues will end; understanding will reach its limit. We know only a portion of the truth, and what we say about God is always incomplete. But when the Complete arrives, our incompletes will be canceled. ¹¹ When I was an infant at my mother's breast, I gurgled and cooed like any infant. When I grew up, I left those infant ways for good. ¹² We don't yet see things clearly. We're squinting in a fog, peering through a mist. But it won't be long before the weather clears and the sun

shines bright! We'll see it all then, see it all as clearly as God sees us, knowing Him directly just as He knows us! ¹³ But for right now, until that completeness, we have three things to do to lead us toward that consummation: Trust steadily in God, hope unswervingly, love extravagantly. And the best of the three is love" I Corinthians 13 The Message.

My challenge is to live by these principles of love. The human spirit of Harold Vann will not encourage me to live by these principles. For this, I must be led by the Holy Spirit. For emphasis, let us review the effect of agape love:

1. In the face of troubles of any sort, I will not give up.
2. I will put God first and others second, including my enemies.
3. I will not envy what you have.
4. I will not brag about what God has given me.
5. I will not be pushy.
6. I will let you take first place.
7. I will hold my temper.
8. I will not let your offenses offend me.
9. I will not brag when you are failing.
10. I will enjoy living the truth.
11. I will not be discouraged.
12. I will trust God's plan.
13. I will be optimistic even when faced by troubles.
14. I will look forward to eternity and not back at my or your failures.

When I mature to the point where I can practice this gift of love fully, I will be spiritually mature. On the way I can still experience joy as discussed in the next chapter.

XII

Joy

Joy means different things to different people. I am joyful when my food is good. I am joyful when my wife is safely home from shopping. I am joyful when we meet with our granddaughters and their children. I am joyful when we see our sons and their families. I am joyful when our son, Roger, visits on Thursdays. I am joyful when the items on the credit card bill are the ones we purchased. There are many joyful things in life.

We will use the word "joy" in the scriptural sense in this study. On searching you find "joy" used in *New Living Translation* 333 times, in *The Message* 124 times, in King James Version 187, in *21st Century King James Version* 184, *American Standard Version* 195 and in *New International Version* 242 times.

The most frequent uses were in terms of celebration and festivals. The other uses were "weeping with joy," "shouting with joy," "dancing with joy," "joy with enthusiasm," "greeting with joy," "singing with joy," "joy in obeying," and as "a joyful city, Jerusalem." Notable scriptures use joy as follows,

> "[3] Some of the traveling teachers recently returned and made me very happy by telling me about your faithfulness and that you are living according to the truth. [4] I could have no greater joy than to hear that my children are following the truth" 3 John 1:3-4 NLT.

And,

> "[4] Peter exclaimed, 'Lord, it's wonderful for us to be here! If you want, I'll make three shelters as memorials—one for you, one for Moses, and one for Elijah.' [5] But even as He spoke, a bright cloud overshadowed them, and a voice from the cloud said, 'This is my dearly loved Son, who brings me great

> joy. Listen to Him.' ⁶ The disciples were terrified and fell face down on the ground" Matthew 17:4-6 NLT.

And again,

> "⁸ The women ran quickly from the tomb. They were very frightened but also filled with great joy, and they rushed to give the disciples the angel's message" Matthew 28:8 NLT.

Peter used the word joy in this description,

> "¹⁷ when he received honor and glory from God the Father. The voice from the majestic glory of God said to him, 'This is my dearly loved Son, who brings me great joy'" 2 Peter 1:17 NLT.

Our challenge is to grow to the point where we find joy not only in pleasurable things but also in our troubles. This is the way we prepare for future troubles which will come. No, we need not go out and look for trouble. It will come.

While editing this section, our electricity went out. With no backup system, I was left with a portion of unsaved text. When the electricity came back, I wrote this as an example and redid some of the work done previously which had not been saved. I am learning again to save frequently. I am joyful to be able to enjoy relearning the wisdom of doing what I have learned in the past. Dealing with our troubles helps us improve

I am joyful that our crime rate has decreased in most cities even though our local newspaper yesterday carried three stories on the front page of serious crimes, including the murder of two people.

It is now time to review why we should be joyful when we meet troubles of various sorts. I am convinced, but I am not yet very consistent in the practice of being joyful. I am still tempted to deny some losses. My memory is not as good as previously, so I need to use assistance in remembering. My challenge is to adjust and not deny.

I am no longer tempted to use bargaining and blaming as much as previously. I am now trying to think "but for the grace of God there I go." Anger is still a problem. I now can get beyond anger easier since my energy (as well as my memory) has decreased. When a driver cuts me off or otherwise bends the rules I become angry. I have not yet developed the habit of praying for him (usually a man.)

Failures often leave me depressed until I can begin to think of my many blessings. My ability to adjust to losses has improved with practice but finding the meaning in my losses continues to challenge me.

God promises me the gifts of faith hope and love. I need to remind myself often by reading His word and praying in order to fully utilize these powerful engines to pull me uphill to joy. If we keep looking and listening, we will find more things over which to be joyful than to be depressed. Please try keeping a list of the blessings you have.

What loss have you had difficulty admitting? Have you lost physical stamina, good health, prestige, your job, love or fortune? God knows you intimately and loves you deeply. He is ready to give you the help you need. You will have to ask him since He does not intrude into your life but is waiting at the door for you to knock. He will let you in and stay with you to the end of your life on earth and then let you in to eternity.

Acknowledgements

Around 20 years ago, I realized that James 1 and later Romans 5 were apparent paradoxes for us as Christians. I wish to thank God for directing Paul and James in writing Romans and James to admonish us to look at losses with an attitude of expecting gain. That paradox was and is a challenge for me. I suspect it will be until my redemption.

I wish to thank Elisabeth Kübler-Ross for her most valuable work in understanding death and describing the process of dealing with death and other losses. If she were still living, I would ask her to read a draft before sending this work to the printers.

I thank God's Holy Spirit who has guided me during this study and writing process. A few weeks after beginning writing, I realized this was too much for me. After resting a few weeks I began to turn it over to His Spirit who dwells in me and from that time have made progress. He has not made me perfect so this work is not perfect.

I am deeply indebted to my wife, Carolyn, who, when she read the very first documentation of this concept, encouraged me. I now thank her for reading the many drafts and for making suggestions on grammar, punctuation and clarity of presentation.

Soon after beginning to realize what James and Paul were saying, I met a friend online, Teresa Bales, who immediately understood this concept and began to relate events in her life and her friends' lives which exemplified the principles. That encouraged me to develop a web page, CopingwithLife.com. She wrote most of the web page from experiences she had lived. I thank Teresa for assisting and encouraging me in this work.

Our son, Roger Vann, with his wide knowledge of people and literature, has been willing to read multiple drafts and make important suggestions for improvements. I thank him deeply.

Our son, Steven Vann, who has a deep understanding of people and of scripture, has been willing to review the drafts. He has given many suggestions for improvement. My thanks to Steven.

I thank our son, Greg Vann, who has read more books than I can count. He understands love better than most people I know. I thank him for reading and suggesting improvements in this work.

I want to thank Tim and Tiffany Ketchum for converting my notes to Power Point several years ago. I have used that presentation regularly, especially with men in their rehabilitation.

A local church of Christ permitted me to present a series of lessons on Wednesday evenings to an adult group which helped me learn to present this concept in an organized way. I especially thank the attendees.

Mike Smith, our adopted son, so to speak, gave me the motivation to go to the local rehab center for a session most weeks of six years to discuss this concept with the men clients. Mike was in our local jail. He requested a visit via the Bible correspondence course he was taking. I reluctantly visited him and recognized his intelligence and his ability to find the truth along with his severe anger. It was difficult to revisit due to his anger but we began corresponding by letter. Soon, it was obvious he was interested in improving. He confessed Jesus Christ as his savior and was baptized. As time progressed he went through rehab. He has married, fathered twins and obtained his Masters Degree and is planning to study for his PhD. He is now the executive officer of a new half-way house for men. I am deeply indebted to him for contributing an important portion of the chapter on meaning. His faith, hope and love have truly lifted him from the depths of despair to joy in his work, family and church. He taught me patience and persistence one more time.

I thank Geoffrey, our minister, and Joanna Sikes, an experienced educator, who each studied a late draft and made suggestions essential in improving this document.

Thanks to Jason Allison, minister to the saints at Pegram, TN, for reviewing a late draft and making important suggestions.

To the men in our local rehab center, I owe a debt for their suffering through my clumsy presentation of this concept an hour at a time during each of their two-to-three-month residence. Their insight and suggestions have been valuable and encouraging.

I want to thank two local Kiwanis clubs and one Civitan club for inviting me to present an overview of this concept to them and for asking questions which caused me to think more clearly before writing this book.

Thanks to Graphics Designs (graphiczxdesigns.zenfolio.com) for being cooperative, efficient and affordable in creating the graphics.

CreateSpace and Amazon.com have been easy to work with in my publishing this work.

Without the assistance of every one of those listed above, it is doubtful that I would have completed this work. I sincerely want to thank each of them.

Please forgive me for any mistakes. They are all mine. Several of the above made suggestions which I did not implement. I was probably wrong in not doing so but I had to decide and I take the blame. I coped to the best of my wisdom.

Harold Vann

The Coping Clock is for your use when you read other materials. Cut it out and use it wherever you desire.

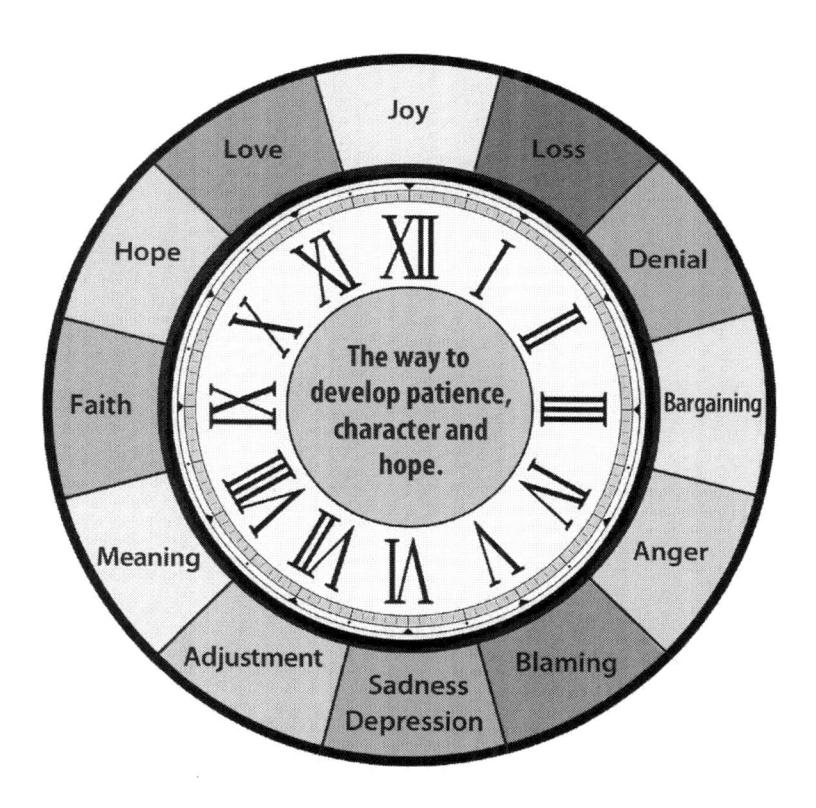

Joy
Love
Loss
Hope
Denial
Faith
Bargaining
The way to develop patience, character and hope.
Meaning
Anger
Adjustment
Blaming
Sadness
Depression

57

Made in the USA
Lexington, KY
07 October 2014